# ARGENTINIAN ADVENTURES

## *A Planthunter in Argentina*

John Lonsdale

To order additional copies of this book, contact:
Xlibris
0800-056-3182
www.xlibrispublishing.co.uk
Orders@ Xlibrispublishing.co.uk

ISBN:  Softcover       978-1-9845-9198-2
       EBook           978-1-9845-9199-9


Print information available on the last page

Rev. date: 10/08/2019

# The First Trip

I found myself in David Cutler's office on the first floor of the Jodrell Laboratory. David is a well-known plant anatomist and tree specialist and one of my previous lecturers. I'd been called there to discuss taking part in an expedition to South America. David had plans to tour Northern Argentina with colleagues from Kew and the Institutio Darwinion in Buenos Aires. This first meeting was in July 1978, a little too soon for me. I felt I was still getting established in my new job at Wakehurst Place.

It was this meeting that resulted in me greeting the others of the team late one evening in September at Gatwick Airport. I had never flown and was a little nervous. But what better way to begin? The others were David; Steve Renvoise, a grass specialist; and Melanie Wilmot-Dear, herbarium assistant and linguist. We were high over the Sussex Weald on our way to a stop at Madrid, where we picked up passengers and refuelled.

Madrid was a disappointment, as it was totally dark when we got there. After about an hour, we were on the way again, flying through the night; next stop, Rio! The journey was enlightened by the usual coffee and peanuts and an irritating film featuring dancing called *Grease*. As dawn began to light the surroundings, I managed to see the Cape Verde Islands slip past way below us.

Then, at last, a coast––we must be near! And so we were. Very soon, the unmistakable figure of Christ appeared briefly as we flew around a surprisingly small sugarloaf. Then we went over more green jungle, before landing at Rio de Janeiro. As soon as we had landed, the doors of the plane were thrown open, and all the smells of the tropics filled the plane. Away in the distance, past clumps of palm trees, the black shapes of vultures could be seen circling in the sky. Later, I learned that they were feasting on the city rubbish dumps. We were in the tropics!

A few passengers disembarked, and we refuelled. We were off again. More green jungle. Nothing ever prepared me for the vast extent of green jungle in South America. We seemed to fly for hours without seeing anything apart from trees, rivers, and occasional wisps of smoke as we followed a very wide river estuary. Then suddenly habitation appeared! We were there! Buenos Aires.

The airport at Buenos Aires was small and very close to the city, so we were soon passing great office buildings and grand shops. We were eventually discharged at a very modest hotel near the main railway station of Retiro. The small hotel where we stayed was probably a Holiday Inn. David liked to book into these. As he rightly said, so much time could be wasted camping out in the wild that it was better to book into a hotel where one existed.

The next few days were spent gathering supplies and meeting our collaborators. One of the first things we did was undertake a walking tour of Buenos Aires. We visited the famous cemetery of La Recoleta and explored famous tourist spots like the plaza de Mayo and the Red

Palace. We also viewed the Torres de Ingleses and the British Tower, which is a copy of Big Ben. Everywhere it was apparent that we were in the tropics. Flamboyant mauve-flowered street trees (*Jacaranda mimosifolia*) and giant kapok trees (*Ceba sp.*) with large seedpods discharging their cotton wool-like contents were everywhere, and the flowering bougainvillea could not be missed. One of the most surprising features was the Transporter Bridge in the Boca. I had seen one before, in Middlesbrough, and was very surprised to see another.

We then had lunch. David would order, as he had a 'little Spanish'. He spent some time telling us about the various cuts of steak and ordered what he thought was *bife de chorizo* for us. After a time, the waiter arrived with a plate of sausages. We looked at him, looked at the plate, and looked back at him. No response. In the end, we decided they were starters and decided to eat them. Then we waited and waited; nothing further came, and we ended lunch without steak!

We left and made our way through the colourful ramshackle houses and restaurants of the Boca. I remember us walking through a flea market and seeing a street photographer with a huge plate camera. We finished the walk by visiting the zoo, where there were herds of a very large mara, capybara-like rodents (*Mara patagonica*), roaming loose in the grounds.

The following day we did the first real work. My job was to locate packing materials for the trip. I remember walking miles through canyon-like warehouses in the commercial section of the city. It wasn't easy finding the obscure supplies necessary for plant collectors. Among the requirements were brown paper; jewellers' tags; adhesive labels; and, most difficult of all, the expanded polystyrene boxes that were to become mobile nurseries. Eventually, these were located at a commercial fishing supplier.

Our next major task was to meet our Argentinian collaborators. The very next morning found us on the way to the suburb of San Isidro where the Instituto Darwinion was based. Here, in a once grand colonial-style building was the herbarium. It was here in the aromatic surroundings of the herbarium that we met the staff, drinking yerba mate, tea made from the Paraguayan holly (*Ilex paraguariensis*) the region is well known for. The tea was served from a silver *bomba* and sucked up through a *bombilla*. I had first heard of yerba mate at Kew, where a nineteenth-century skin of a giant anteater stuffed with it still resided under a table in Dilly's office!

Among the people I met in the herbarium was the director, A.L. Cabrera, a distinguished old-school gentleman. Some of the younger members of staff made fun of his Castilian accent (people don't use the Spanish 'lisp' in Argentina). I also met the cactus expert Roberto Keesling, and I remember a lady from La Plata who I think was his wife. Later she was to show us the Museum of the University of La Plata, where some of the most interesting and grisly exhibits were the desiccated mummies from the High Andes.

We were then introduced to what would be our transport for the next three months. It was a Chevrolet Four-Track, four-wheel drive with a limited differential–ideal for the job.

Formalities complete, we set off in the evening of 31 October. After driving for a while, we began to see strange groups of people wearing masks and carrying lighted candles. We were told they were gathered at cemeteries. This was somewhat unsettling, until we were told that this was the Day of the Dead. People celebrated in this way every year.

We eventually reached Salta Grande, our first collecting site, situated adjacent to the Uruguay River, where a huge hydroelectric dam was being constructed. On arrival we had a meal and gratefully retired to bed.

The next morning, we were given a tour of the dam. This involved a trip across the river to Uruguay. The dam was enormous and was still incomplete. We were taken down several floors via exposed steel ladders to the turbine hall to see the generators being fitted. Everything was on a giant scale. Any one of the many discharge pipes would easily have coped with the largest UK river.

But back to why we were there––plant collecting. In the grounds of the hotel, I made our very first collection. It was of a very attractive small purple flower that grew in the lawns. It was identified as *Alophia amoena* in the family Iridaceae, although now it is known as *Herbertia lahue*. David required multiple collections for his research. So I quickly made six collections and established them in a temporary nursery in one of our polystyrene boxes.

A few more of our first collections were made here. A short distance away, from above the river, I spotted an interesting Bromeliad with curled silver-grey foliage. This was *Tillandsia caput-medusae*. Alongside this was a small species, possibly *Tillandsia bryoides* now (*Tillandsia multiflora*), a plant we would see for the next few thousand miles north, growing on telegraph lines. Also here was a pendulous species of the cactus *Cereus*, another species of which I would find as a twenty-foot plant with a tree form, in sparse dry woodland nearby. The most attractive plant found in this area was an orchid in the genus *Miltonia* with large pale greenish cream flowers.

Our small group was gathered in a grassy dry area. We were being shown the boyhood home of General San Martin, who had freed Argentina from Spanish rule in 1822. We were staying at a Hotel of Automobile Espania–the equivalent of our AA. It was a pleasant hotel not far from the Guarani River.

As soon as we arrived, we found our rooms and set up the plant driers on the steps of the hotel. We wandered over to the riverbank to see what we could find. We hadn't been there many minutes when we were startled by people shouting, 'Fuego!' 'Fuego!' 'Hotel fuego!' And so it was. Looking back, we could see clouds of smoke coming from the hotel. The plant driers had caught fire! I had thought that the paraffin burners seemed rather dangerous but thought that herbarium people would know this, and it was before the days of risk assessment. Close examination of the damage revealed a rather scorched hotel porch and a pile of smouldering newspapers containing valuable specimens. The herbarium team began the depressing work of salvaging specimens. Amazingly, not much was lost (compressed newspaper is surprisingly noncombustible). Perhaps even more surprisingly, we were allowed to stay the night!

I resumed my forage for plants and found some scruffy hedges in which was an interesting bright orange flowered climber with spiky leaves and daisy-like flowers, *Mutisia*. There was also a mass of climbing foliage and tendrils with small white flowers and plum-like fruits, a species of *Passiflora*, or passion flower. Another interesting plant was a small tree about the size of a crab apple but carrying large bright pink pea-like flowers. This proved to be the national flower of Argentina, *Erithrina crista-galli*. In the grass, there were pink and white trumpets of *Zepheranthes* species. We would have more bulbs for our collection.

As we moved through Entre Rios, we found it to be mostly grassland punctuated with spires of red earth, termite mounds. It also turned out to be one of the best places for birdwatching that one could ever hope to find. One of the most intriguing birds left evidence of its nests at regular intervals. These nests, made of red lateritic mud and shaped into covered structures like the domed ovens seen in many village houses, give it the common name ovenbird. Also emerging from the grass were very tall thistle-like plants, which were a species of *Erygium*. Perched on the telegraph wires were various hawks and *Caracara* species, which made birdwatching from the vehicle an interesting pursuit.

I recall a memorable collecting stop where we gathered plants by a pool. And again I found plants I had only seen in the hothouses of Kew. In particular, I found a climbing species of *Thunbergia*, with lilac flowers with darker veins. The rich scarlet crest of a bird could not be mistaken for any other than the cock-of-the-rock (*Andean Rupicola peruvianus*). It was here I first saw a water hyacinth (*Eichhornia azurea*), a close relative of the more familiar *E. crassipes* which we collected in flower. It can still be seen flowering at Kew each summer.

The next stop I remember was Three Hills. These three low hills are the highest points for miles, making them notable features. It was on these rocky raised points that I collected three species of *Hippeastrum, H. rutilans* and two others. I also collected a densely spined cactus, *Rebutia* spp.

Around this time, we were accommodated at a very rural ranch. In reality, it was just a cluster of mud-floored agricultural buildings surrounded by a few willow and eucalyptus trees with a small flock of very aggressive turkeys in the yard.

Our next stop was a large estancia. What a contrast! The place had comfortable rooms and a *laguna* outside. David and the others decided to swim in the cool water. I didn't swim, so I took advantage of a small boat we'd been given the use of. I collected several species of aquatic plants, including *Cabomba* and three *Salvinia* species, before seeing through the very clear water the unmistakable shapes of piranha beneath. Swimming now didn't seem nearly so attractive!

We travelled to the far north-east of Argentina, Misiones province, where our next stop was just as comfortable. We were housed in an agricultural college managed by Jesuit priests, in the middle of delightfully scented orange plantations. Our visit coincided with graduation day and an enormous *asado* was being prepared, Parents were arriving in cars and staking claim to huge piles of meat, which had been killed and butchered on the premises. It was later grilled on sticks over thirty foot long trenches filled with glowing charcoal. Walking though the acres of fragrant oranges was a treat, as was picking kumquats in the blazing sunshine. There was not a lot to collect on that estate, but I did find a large red spidery *Hippeastrum* species growing in a bog. Despite the bog being two feet deep, I managed to extract it, and it was sent to Kew.

Much of the natural habitat had been converted to agriculture and forestry, *Pinus caribaea*, with its strange foxtail-like malformed terminal growths, and eucalyptus covered most of the available land.

It was forestry that supported our next stop. We were given access to a Celulosa Argentina guest house at Puerto Piray. This was positively luxurious and came fully stocked with cold drinks and staff who came in to clean and prepare food. Here we made many collections in the rainforest, including the delicate orchid *Epidendrum argentiniana*. High points of our stay were finding a rhinoceros beetle in the garden and the myriad of butterflies in the nearby jungle, including masses of swallowtails at riverside salt licks. There was also the multicoloured heliconius butterfly, which would rest on our arm or head, and the occasional large metallic blue morpho, which glided along shady streams.

It was in this guest house that I read an article in a travel magazine about the Andes. It was planned that we would reach the foothills, but photographs of llamas convinced me that we must see the Andes proper. We were taken to meet some forest officers, one of whom stood out as the unhappiest man in the nation. He seems to have been an academic, until some political shenanigans had him transferred to practical work deep in the forest. This was not his natural habitat. He was decidedly not happy.

From here, we took time out to visit the great waterfall of Iguaçu. This was tremendous, the more so as it was almost in flood at the time. From the falls, you can look over to where three countries––Argentina, Brazil, and Paraguay––meet.

We had the opportunity of visiting Paraguay and took the ferry from Posadas to enter a town apparently from another age. Most transport seemed to be by horse. There were small horse-driven carts everywhere. These and masses of eight-year-old kids trying to sell visitors tins of Tiger balm were the only memorable parts of the excursion––no plants.

Other interesting excursions we had made were more fruitful. The first, a walk over a bridge into Concordia, Brazil, was notable for the nightjars we saw feeding on moths hovering near the street lights and, secondly, the immediate change of atmosphere in Brazil! Everywhere there was music playing loudly in the streets. From where, we couldn't tell. It was quite a change from solid sensible Argentina. Back in sensible Argentina, we visited the ruins of the Jesuit monastery at San Isidro.

Argentina was, however, not so sensible. It was going through changes that we knew nothing about. We were aware of constantly being stopped on the roads and of the nervous response of our guides to the gun-toting officials who stopped us. We were assured that these were just provincial police and occasional federal checks––despite being held at gunpoint while they checked our papers. There was the odd mention of rebels, which we didn't understand. It was only after we were back in the United Kingdom that we learned how troubled Argentina had been during these years (it was the peak of the years of the *los desaparecidos*) and how lucky we had been not to have been involved.

Our collecting moved on via Corrientes, where I saw nothing but the herbarium. My job was examining the collections made so far and posting some to Kew. From here, we continued higher in the Andean foothills and eventually got to Tucuman, where we stayed in an unnervingly depopulated university high over the town.

Then we were on to Salta. Salta, how I remember Salta. We had just entered town when, suddenly, the vehicle was struck from behind. From my position in the back of the truck, I could clearly see that we had been hit by a police car. Everyone was nervous now, as we remembered the roadside checks and guns. The police insisted on taking our driver to the police station, even though the collision was clearly not our fault.

After an interminable wait, the driver was released, and all was well.

We had begun our return journey, but there was still much to see. We came to an area where there was a constant stream of high-sided trucks carrying bamboo-like stems. This unexpected crop was sugar cane, and it was a delight to see this tropical plant. The sugar workers didn't seem to be well paid, and their accommodation in barrack-style temporary villages left much to be desired. Interesting, but not desirable.

We were in the foothills of the Andes. But still determined to see llama, we had to press on. And so we did. We were now in the far north-west, just inland of the Pacific and one of the most botanically interesting areas we would visit. Higher in the Andes, in the land of painted mountains, we reached the town of Humahuaca. At this height, we eventually began to see llama. One personal aim was fulfilled. It was another opportunity for sightseeing while collecting.

We took a side road even higher in the Andes and eventually emerged on a plateau between Argentina and Chile, in which were the salt pans of the Salinas Grande. In this white salt desert, we saw Guanacos and wind devils (small tornados). Extremely dwarf cushion plants were very interesting. They showed several families of plants responding to the conditions in the same way (convergent evolution). We passed through a reserve of *Trichocereus pasacana*, the largest cactus in Argentina, which can reach thirty feet high. Later at Volcan, I would collect the world's smallest cactus, *Blossfeldia liliputiana*, less than an inch high!

From here on, it seemed there was a new species of cactus every half mile. On the western, wetter sides of the hills were flowering shrubs and trees with epiphytes covering their branches. Here I found the brilliant red *Fuchsia boliviensis*, the yellow *Nicotiana glauca*, and the violet blue tubular flowers of *Iochroma cyaneum*.

It was here also that I discovered the joys of travelling as a passenger on narrow mountain tracks driven by a seemingly suicidal Kew driver. From my outpost in the back of the Four-Track, I could look down on a rear wheel being kept four-inches from a precipitous drop of a few hundred feet. A shout at the driver helped regain more normal road sense.

After days of cactus collecting, relieved only by the odd bulb of *Zephyranthes*, we decided that we were due another outing. And as we were in the far north of Argentina, we would go for a day in Bolivia. So we made our way to the village of La Quiaca, where it was possible to walk over the border to Villazón. Walking over the border was done by way of a causeway built into the desert. It was just a raised sand platform built over a drainage channel.

At the border, we met no one! All that was there was a notice that said, in Spanish, 'Gone to lunch'! Lunch was very prolonged, so it was quite late in the afternoon as we wandered down a desert-dry tired street and found a nineteenth century style hotel. Not being over enamoured with the vintage accommodation, we ate and settled down for the night. But what a night. No sooner had I put my head down to sleep, there was a huge bang and then another and another, nonstop. All of our party looked worried. And we should have been. The next morning we found that Argentina had gone on a war footing with Bolivia, and the respective armies had amused themselves by firing field guns over the border at each other all night.

We made our way to Molinos via the highest pass in South America. From this high point, the road snakes down the Valle Calchaquí, a valley of incomparable views. We were heading for the region of Catamarca, and from here, things got a lot more agricultural as we progressed through the winemaking region of Catamarca. We were all very tired and urgently looking forward to getting back to the United Kingdom. Serious collecting had been abandoned. We'd been on the road three months and would eventually cover over ten thousand kilometres.

We would rush back to Buenos Aires. Occasionally we would still collect from the vehicle. This was one of these occasions. I spotted a four-foot high lily growing in a roadside ditch and jumped out and collected it. It was later identified as *Canna glauca*.

Another memorable plant collected at this late stage was a very prostrate purple-flowered roadside plant looking much like a verbena. I spotted it while we were doing about 50 miles per hour, stopped the truck, and ran back to gather seed. Well worth stopping for, the plant was identified back at Kew as *Glandularia pulverulenta* and, in time, became quite a popular and useful summer bedding plant.

# The Second Trip
## 12 November 2003

Twenty-five years later, to the day, I was back, travelling past the strangely familiar red cliffs of Angosto de Prechel, where we'd collected the world's smallest cactus, *Blossfeldia liliputana*. In 1978, the road from Salta had been the usual dusty, rutted stone surface. A brightly painted diesel engine thundered past. I'd remembered every detail of our arrival at Tilcara––pulling into a roadside stop, shaded by the poplars and willows that announce habitation everywhere in Argentina. After purchasing comestibles at a tiny local shop, we enjoyed a picnic lunch of bread, cheese, and tinned corned beef, almost liquid in the scorching sun.

The only evidence of the passing of a quarter of a century was the unexpected and welcome smooth tarmac road and the bent, corroded rails of the railway, which once had run half the length of a continent, abandoned in the financial ruin of the 1980s. The valley is famous for its spectacular 'painted' geology. Luxury coaches now daily disgorge flocks of tourists. Few venture beyond Puchara, the restored Indian fortress, the restaurants and souvenir shops of Tilcara, and the picturesque whitewashed town of Humahuaca a few miles to the north, close to the Bolivian border.

*Valley near Tilcara*

We drive into town, our pallid blue Chrysler Corsa, quite a contrast to the rugged four-wheel drive Chevrolet of the last visit. In a cobbled side street just off the Spanish-style square, the hotel is of the 'adequate' variety. The sleeping quarters are a series of small rooms around a tiny courtyard. We squeeze past a loud, outsize, bossy female tour guide as the hotelier tells her, 'It's far too dry for mosquitoes.'

A night behind a door so warped that an armadillo could have walked through quickly disproved his mosquito theory. Next morning, one eye completely closed and the other only 10 per cent open gave a new outlook on life and an interesting appreciation of the effects of allergic reactions!

Of course all the usual tourist stuff had to be done: Visit the ruins and the local archaeological museum. Bargain for souvenirs from the disinterested stallholders with their identical range of handmade llama products! But away from this, behind innominate doors, lurked wonderful emporia extinct from our sterile shopping centres. Here were real shops with real stock. They held mousetraps, mothballs, coffee pots, radios, batteries, glue, string––and not just string, a selection of string––cord, yarn, and rope. Here was everything you needed and more, in a great, confused stack and jumble of which only the elderly assistant could ever know the full extent.

A bar with no beer. Night. Another meal, carne de bife, another bar. We had a choice of an open-windowed hovel festooned with local youth high on sixties pop or a dimly lit restaurant inhabited by a nervous-looking owner practising panpipes, drum, and guitar with three kids of assorted ages and sizes. The smallest was despatched to bring *cerveza*, seemingly a scarce commodity on the premises. The others waited anxiously in case the miniscule messenger was hijacked by predatory youth. It wasn't clear what they could have done, but the kid was a survivor and soon dodged back out of the shadows. Drinks sorted, practising resumed; we were forgotten. Music flowed from the older members. The youngest, chivvied into demonstrating his skill on pipes and drums, was teased whenever he missed a note. It seemed the owner was a famous player; the walls proudly displayed his collection of faded newspaper cuttings.

On the road again. It was a perfect morning––bright, cool, the bluest of skies, seeming clearer than anywhere else on earth. The air, filtered by a 6,000-mile Pacific voyage, had had its last dust particles washed out in the final giddy ascent of the Andes. Leaving Tilcara we'd asked if the road was OK for the Corsa.

'Yes, it's a good road.'

'Good' must have been a relative term. Lulled into a false sense of security by the smooth black surface, we turned right to reality at Pumahuaca, where crushed stone replaces tarmacadam. Much of the time, it was a benign, if dusty, surface, reflecting the geology of the immediate surroundings. But at intervals, it became bad tempered and showed its rocky teeth. This was an ancient road, a pre-Columbian desert highway to the Salinas Grandes, the crossroads to Chile, Bolivia, and Peru.

At 4,000 metres, high on the altiplano, the Salinas present the weirdest landscape. Glistening salt shimmers into the distance over the vestiges of a vast dry lakebed. A constant mirage reflects the mountains, tricking the unwary into a pointless search for water. Rain may not have fallen here for years. Scrubby puna vegetation supports small herds of llama, alpaca, sheep, and donkeys. In this intramontane basin, only the deepest-rooted plants survive, drawing up subterranean moisture supplemented by night-time mists. The desiccating heat of the day causes dust devils to perform their crazy gyrations through stiff tussocks of sulphur-gold grasses and sclerotic green mounds of cushion plants––unbelievably, the distant relatives of carnation and carrot. 'Puna' also describes a potentially fatal altitude sickness. Acclimatise; move slowly. The local people have more red corpuscles in their blood than lowlanders. Altitude sickness is no fun.

*Flowering cushion plant (Caryophyllaceae sp.)*

We traversed fifty miles of salt flats, passing abandoned crumbling fortress-like way stations and groups of supercilious llamas. They always seem to have a great opinion of themselves. A huge pebble cartouche high on a scree slope announces our arrival at San Antonio de Los Cobres, the name spelt out starkly in bleached white rocks. It was a frontier town if ever there was one, founded on copper mining in the nineteenth century. Adobe houses, dogs, dust, and schoolkids. Dated North American pop music blasted from windows, but it was a place to pause, relax, and refuel. There was all a traveller needed––passable restaurants; basic essentials, water and fuel; and a local 'gomería'. How we would need a gomería. But that would be later.

Leaving under a cloud, we found it surprising how much dust a Corsa could create! The road stretched out straight and flat to a disappearing point twenty miles ahead, where mountains punctuated the haze. To the west, the highest peaks of the Andes, snow-topped at 20,000 feet, separated Argentina from Chile. The occasional vehicles we'd seen on the approach to San Antonio de los Cobres headed west to high mountain passes and on to Chile. But for us, it was south, following a line of tottering telegraph poles, bumping over the rough road towards the 18,500-foot Nevado de Acay (the Snowed One of Acay) and Abra del Acay, the highest navigable pass in South America.

*Llama near San Antonio de los Cobres*

Suddenly, perhaps predictably, rock pierced rubber; a rear tyre rapidly deflated. The sensible thing to do was to return to town. But we had a spare and an optimistic outlook, and our destination, Cachi, seemed not too far away! Tyre changed. Onward we went, rising from the plain into foothills overlooking a rolling valley. Guanacos, elegant sandy gold wild relatives of llama, grazed rough grass and Baccharis scrub. Baccharis are some of the most boring plants in the world, low shrubs in the daisy family. Boring as they may be, they're successful! Four hundred species cover thousands of square miles of arid South America.

## Guanaco Country

Cresting the summit, a signboard proudly displayed the altitude, 4,850 metres (almost 16,000 feet). Below, a grassy gorge plunged steeply, and the road began its tortuous decent.

Pssst, pssst, pssst, pssst! Each revolution of the front nearside wheel hissed unwelcome news––another puncture! Two burst tyres, high altitude desert, half litre of water, a pineapple, and handful of sweets––it wasn't the recommended survival strategy for our situation! OK. Stop. Wait. Stay with the car. A passing vehicle will soon assist. We waited, stationary, on a blind bend, on a mountain road, a 500-foot drop on one side, an unstable overhanging cliff on the other, my travelling companion with a blinding high-altitude headache. It didn't take long to decide that this was not ideal. Nor did it take long to realise we'd not seen a vehicle travelling in either direction for the last thirty miles––not even a dust cloud in the far distance!

An hour of waiting passed. We checked out the mountain. Ahead were endless contortions as the road doubled back on itself time and time again, losing a few hundred feet each time. 'What the!'

A grey shape half a metre long bounded from the cliff above my head, tail streaming in mid-air. It crossed the road in one bound, turned, stared straight back at me with an unnerving human-like face––huge dark forward-facing eyes and pink elfin ears glowing translucent in the setting sun. In a second, it was gone, bounding out of sight over the precipitous edge. Wow! Though it looked like a gremlin, chinchilla came to mind. Were they from the Andes? Weren't they the stupid torpid balls of grey that snoozed in Pets Are Us? This one wasn't; it was an animated streak of silver going somewhere in a hurry! Minutes later, another followed using the same well-worn track. It seemed we'd stumbled onto a chinchilla highway.

Our conclusion after reconnoitring the road––not good. It was rocky, rutted, and strewn with fierce tyre piercers. Tracks confirmed that other vehicles did come this way. But how often? Tracks could persist for weeks in these arid conditions. Late afternoon, the sun dipped inevitably to the horizon, its light beautiful. Shadows slid over the valleys. Forget the photographs. We had to get out of this place. Revised plan––nearest village, La Poma, thirty miles away and thousands of feet below. At this altitude, desiccating days and freezing nights ruled out walking unless fully prepared. We weren't. Half a litre of water and a pineapple; I don't think so!

How far could you go on a flat tyre? I didn't know but joyriders in police documentaries seemed to be able to go for miles and at great speed too. Maybe not on these roads however!

With one driving, one walking, we went at a snail's pace. The walker kicked away the worst stones and guided the driver away from ruts. It seemed to work. But the road zigzagging down the mountain did not help. Counting down the roadside markers, three concertinaed kilometres produced about one kilometre of forward direction. At each turn, the tyre squeaked and squealed, desperate to be free from its rim. At each turn, we winced and wondered how long it could be restrained.

We went six kilometres, as if following the man with a red flag walking in front of a vintage car. Good––six kilometres and the tyre still on. It was getting darker now. We decided to risk it, put as much weight into the back as possible (including the passenger who'd given up red flag duty) and roll on. Our average speed increased to six miles per hour!

The road got worse the lower we got. There was water down here. It had washed gullies into the surface. In the dark, we hit a ford, not deep but rocky. Soon after, a metallic noise told us it was all over for this tyre. We had another. It was flat, but it was still on the rim! Tyre one had lasted sixteen kilometres. Fingers crossed, tyre two should get us to civilisation.

Putting a flat tyre on a car in the dark by the light of a pencil torch was a novel experience–– interesting but not recommended! In the pitch-dark, we continued. We came to another ford, bigger this time, the rushing water audible before the headlights picked it up. My travelling companion was getting nervous now. Something about the 'depth of unknown waters in the dark'.

One more ford successfully negotiated proving 'you can take a Corsa to water and not get stuck in the drink'.

My companion, now more agitated: 'It's no joke.'

Fording streams was banned for the night.

Under the stars, don't try kipping in a Corsa. General Motors may have banged on about how comfortable the beast was, but it was a diurnal creature! At night, sharp pointy bits sprouted from nowhere, padding lost its resilience, and space contracted like a dying star entering a black hole. There was no way to get comfortable. And it was cold, very cold.

What with the cold and the pointy bits, it was a relief when, at last, the sky turned inky blue and dawn began to illuminate the mountain ridges. At 6 a.m. half-light, cold, crisp, and clear, we were eighteen miles from the nearest village. And walking was still not an attractive prospect. But hey! We still had three wheels.

It was light now. One more ford, a bumpy push through a seriously rocky gorge, and we emerged above the river. Below, in the river valley, emerald-green patches showed there was cultivation, and cultivation meant people.

We travelled only three kilometres before we heard dogs barking. There was smoke ahead and a rustic farmstead. Help at last? A derelict old Peugeot reclined in the shade of a tree alongside the low adobe dwelling. Its once crimson paintwork, long ago weathered to patchy red ochre, was now buried under strata of dust. It seemed an unlikely recovery vehicle, but we thought we'd try. Two similarly ancient Indian women fussed around the yard ignoring our attempts to engage them with our 'problema de auto' or 'goma de auto desinflado'. A perfectly reasonable response if you care for the Spanish language! They obviously didn't care for strange gringos and shuffled rapidly away.

Two more kilometres ahead, poplars and willows appeared in the distance––habitation! Better still, a radio mast! We limped towards a small school. Its freshly painted white fence posts contrasted strongly with the red-and-purple mountain beyond. From a small chapel came the sound of children singing. We entered the open door of the school and found two nuns preparing food for the morning break. After we'd quickly recounted our tale of 'problema de auto' and 'goma de auto desinflado,' water and coffee were proffered. Yes, there was radio contact with the outside world; help would be at hand when the teacher finished morning service.

'How many vehicles pass each day?' we asked.

'None' was the sobering reply.

We could have still been waiting at 16,000 feet.

One, two, and then three sun-browned faces peered nervously through the door. A crowd of excited kids rushed in to see their outlandish visitors. A smiling round-faced adult in a white lab coat was introduced as the head teacher (and part-time radio operator). He was a practical man, used to fixing things with the minimum of resources. A handyman was sent for, and in no time, the wheel was off the car and the tyre off the rim.

Now we had a Corsa with three wheels and a jack. Not a great improvement! But they'd fix the tyre. How? That was far less clear.

The interior of the tyre had a developed a spaghetti-like quality and contained a pound of rubber dust. This car was going no further.

Radio La Poma. Get help.

OK, in theory.

'Poma, Poma, Poma.'

*Crackle, hiss,* nothing.

'Poma, Poma, Poma.'

*Hiss, crackle.*

'Poma, Poma, Poma.'

Nothing.

'Poma, Poma, Poma.'

*Crackle, crackle, hiss,* nothing.

'Poma, Poma, Poma.'

A quarter of an hour later, still nothing. Retune to other stations.

'Cachi, Cachi, Cachi.'

'Salta, Salta, Salta.'

'Molinos, Molinos, Molinos.'

All had their own unique combination of hisses, squeaks, and crackles.

At last, there came a response from Molinos, who would try to raise La Poma.

Twenty minutes later, La Poma had been contacted, but the result was lost in translation.

Another plan was hatched. The wind-creased handyman, resembling one of the less desirable characters from a Clint Eastwood film, was despatched up the road––we assumed for a puncture repair kit. *Some hope!* we thought. We were in the company of nuns. Maybe powers beyond our understanding were at work?

Whilst we waited, the schoolchildren took us on a tour of the school. They understood that we were strange 'botanicos' and were keen to show us their herb garden, chickens, and pigs. They were learning about global change, conservation and sustainability. These kids from a tiny population, living in harmony with their surroundings, were more aware than most Western urban consumers of the fragility of the environment.

*Herb garden*

Instead of a handyman, a thundercloud returned, emitting bangs, splutters, and coughs. Unbelievably, as the dust subsided, a familiar ochre-red shape emerged. These were the last remains of a vehicle that we'd have bet parked for the last time a decade ago. If you took it onto a European road, it would probably result in arrest.

The engine didn't like being woken. More accurately, the two and a half cylinders that were firing didn't like it. Only a large rock on the accelerator kept it running. If it stopped, three people were needed to bump-start it. We eventually understood that, unlikely as it seemed, this 'car' would transport our tyre for repair. It would take not only our tyre but also ourselves and our luggage to La Poma. As the Peugeot's tyres seemed in nearly as ruinous a state as ours, its gears no longer meshed, and the brakes seemed to rely on the power of prayer, this was not an attractive prospect.

Saying goodbye, the nuns treated us as if they were seeing off old friends, not strangers they'd met two only hours ago. They were good people. After a group photograph of the children and with a wave of hands, we were off and into the clutches of the Clint Eastwood renegade and his rusty steed.

*Farewell*

Some of the roughest road so far came just beyond the school. Only the innate skill of the driver, who was able to wrestle unwilling steering, stamp on ineffective brakes, and double declutch at the same time got us through. Untroubled by the death rattles and shudders of the recalcitrant engine, the driver pulled in at a roadside dwelling. Stopping seemed unwise. Going was what we preferred!

Errand complete, we move on. The old 'rock on the accelerator trick' had worked again. Just as well. There was no chance of bump-starting a car in this terrain.

We'd covered hardly any distance when we stopped again. The driver offered a hitchhiker a lift to town in a car that was ready for its last rites and already bulging with wheels, tyres, passengers, and suitcases. To our relief, the lady took fright at seeing strange foreigners and declined the offer, preferring a fifteen-mile walk to a lift with these dangerous people.

We settled into the journey, uneventful and pleasant now, following the course of the river, passing patches of cultivation where women tended sheep and worked their fields. The mountains rose on all sides, spectacular scenery. A flock of green Andean conures swooped into a roadside tree, their indigo wings flashing like damascened steel in the morning sun.

*Tending the flock*

La Poma was not on our itinerary. In the normal course of events, we'd have passed right by. It would have hardly registered. But here we were in town. Admittedly, it was a very small town, but a town true to itself, not a tourist stop (too small for much disturbance), going about its business in a quiet timeless way. We knew there was a *hosteria* and we'd heard there was a gomería, a repairer of tyres. We found the hostería. We found the gomería. What we didn't find were tyres!

'Ola.' Juan, our charming silver-haired hotelier, sporting a jaunty scarlet neckerchief, welcomed us and quickly arranged rooms, a meal, and drinks. We soon discovered that 'quickly' was what Juan did! This silver-haired man in his sixties did everything at speed. He had a ready smile, a wry sense of humour, and a conspiratorial wink whenever he disagreed, usually with those younger than himself!

Juan had been in conversation when we arrived. His companion, David, was swiftly summoned to translate for the 'Ingleses'. David, David La-Poma. Was this really his surname? His ancestors had been rich landowners who'd settled here at the time of the Spanish conquest. Even now, he owned thousands of acres of mountainside, but proving title seemed a lifelong quest. David was a veritable walking history of La Poma.

We explained how we'd arrived and impressed everyone with our story of our 'problema de auto' and 'dormido en la noche del la montaña' (although, at the time, our translation was not so advanced!).

Two threads now began––the great recovery and an intensive induction into four hundred years of pre- and post-Hispanic history. In between, there was a wandering German biscuit maker, adventures with the police, and 'the five great promises of assistance'.

Let's start with the biscuit maker, the only other guest. An elderly German chef de patisserie, he domiciled in Australia and was travelling South America by bus. Brooking no protest, he'd invaded the kitchen, produced enough biscuits for two days, and then vanished on the two o'clock *colectivo*. Did he do this everywhere? Strange man, nice biscuits, strange mission!

The only telephone in town was supervised by a bored girl in a booth, her days brightened by eavesdropping. Hire company contacted, a recovery vehicle was promised for 6 p.m. They'd phone back later to confirm. Promise one!

Immediate problem solved, David began an intensive history tour. An intensive rest would have been more welcome after a night on the mountain, but the tour was fascinating.

The roads we'd travelled were part of a pre-Incan network reaching from the distant past. At one point 'El Camino Real' (the Inca Royal Way), a pre-Incan road and the modern road can be all be seen at different levels of the hillside. Drystone walls mark the Camino Real. There'd been walls at either side but only one remains intact. The other became a convenient source of building material. Four hundred years later, Incan walls still defined field boundaries, and their sacred menhirs (standing stones) ensured fertility. High above the valley, white stones visible for miles, marked routes to safe mountain passes and long abandoned mines, the source of Incan gold.

*David on the 'Camino Real'*

David knew all this. He'd lived his life in the mountains. He was a mountaineer and guide. He talked of wildlife and solitude and the giant condor that scared travellers from its territory, following close overhead, trapping them in its magnified shadow. Some of his stories were tragic. Drunks would ride horses into the mountains and not be missed. Rescuers would find their frozen bodies days later. Once, he'd revived a near-dead climber with his own body heat, got his heart beating again, wrapped him in a space blanket, and carried him miles down the mountainside, only to find he'd frozen to death on the way. His enduring regret––'he was only a boy.'

We returned to the hostería. Had there been confirmation from the rescue service? 'No call.'

Juan would ring again. Off he went, running across the square. Running was his thing; walking was too slow––this despite his dire warnings of the dangers of exertion at high altitude.

'Nada'––no confirmation.

We rang again. There'd been a delay. The vehicle would arrive 'tomorrow morning' (promise two).

No great problem. This was a pleasant place to stay, offering good food and an evening's conversation. A description in broken Spanish and a rough sketch of the elfin-eared creature brought gasps.

'Yes, yes, animal puesto en peligro, chinchilla, how lucky to see one.'

'Dos' I said.

'Two?!' Doubly lucky! 'Climbers spend years in the mountains and never see chinchilla.'

They were that scarce, hunted almost to extinction in the early years of the twentieth century.

As we talked, the sky turned grey, and there was a spectacular lightning flash followed by rolling thunder. There'll be rain, we said.

'No. It's two years since we had rain, but there will be snow in the mountains.'

*Mountains from La Poma*

Early morning, the mountains were clothed with snow, gold and pink in the morning light. Acay now really was the Snowed One. From the point where we'd stopped, a blanket of snow reached down three thousand feet. At the appointed time—no truck, nothing.

We rang the rescue company. 'There's been heavy rain in Salta. All services are at full stretch. There'll be someone there this afternoon. We'll ring to confirm the time' (promise three).

They didn't!

Things were getting edgy now. Promises were getting thin. Another phone call produced evasive answers. Doubt that Corsas were covered for journeys into the Altiplano. No mention of this was made when we hired, but there are doubts now! Buried in tiny Spanish print, there may be an admonition not to take this route.

David got involved. 'Disgrace.' 'Threat to our tourist industry.' 'No way to treat visitors.'

Continuing a rising cascade of pressure, we were assured, 'This will get action.'

Not so sure, we went along. It was Argentina after all, and they had ways of their own. We, however, had a flight to meet, with international connections and thirty-six hours to make it. The countdown had begun.

David's talked his way out of the small print. The recovery vehicle would come, but it would take six hours (promise four).

Nothing more to be done but hang around, read a book.

It didn't come.

Juan winked and gave a look that said, 'I knew it wouldn't.'

David took a new approach. In the square, the police were taking the air outside the station. Since our arrival, we'd known they were watching our situation—not overtly involved, just observing in the background. David got them out of the background.

The chief of police would 'contact our guys in Molinos' three hours away. He did. They found tyres. 'They'll bring them over. They'll set off after lunch.' (promise five) Great, problem solved!

But soon a mysterious change came. The police were no longer coming. This didn't sound so good!

It seemed that Juan had realised there'd be a quicker way, and time was short.

Back in the telephone booth, he'd negotiated with the tyre dealers in Molinos. It had been tricky. They had no new tyres, but they had second-hand ones. They'd bring them but needed payment first. How? Eventually a deal was struck. The tyres would arrive by taxi!

Sure enough, midafternoon, a taxi arrived. Promise five, fulfilled! Another minor miracle, the taxi looked and sounded just like the Peugeot of yesterday and in similar condition. And it had tyres. Nine of them! Four on the wheels and five inside, for us. Not one of the nine would be legal anywhere in the world! We selected two with the fewest holes, no point checking for tread! I set off for the gomería to have one fitted to the wheel we'd brought with us. No one seemed concerned that our tyre had been low profile, and these were four inches wider.

The taxi drove off. This confused us. We had an inflated tyre in La Poma and a Corsa on the mountain. How would we get them together?

Another of Juan's deals came into play. It involved the police again. They had a large, impressive, very shiny four-wheel drive truck. The chief of police had duties to attend to, one of which would take him past our school. Into the truck we piled––ourselves, the police chief, David, and his small son. At the school, we disembarked.

The police chief immediately drove off. This seemed a rash overconfident and premature departure. There were three wheels on the car, thankfully still inflated, and worryingly, a much larger wheel in our hands.

Eventually we proved there was room for a full-size tyre in the Corsa's wheel arch. Just as well! Tyre on, one corner of the car higher than the other hardly seemed to affect the handling. Safely back in town, we headed to the gomería and the second geriatric tyre was fitted to the spare wheel. At last, we had a full complement of tyres, but confidence in their durability was zero.

It was late afternoon. Was there time to get to Cachi tonight? We were nervous now. Driving into the night on unreliable tyres was not appealing; we knew what the roads could do.

The need to get to Salta for tomorrow's flight made our decision. We pressed on. More rocky road, more mountains––the road seemed to go on forever––but eventually in the dusk, the lights of Cachi were below us.

It was a pretty seventeenth-century town of cobbled streets; at its centre was a Spanish-style square, shaded by palms and an impressive whitewashed church. At night it was lively, its windows and doorways blazed with light. People thronged the streets, tourists and locals alike, shopping and visiting restaurants. We pulled in for the night and a well-deserved rest.

The hostería was a recently refurbished ACA (Argentinian Automobile Association). In 1978, it would have been generous to describe it as clean and comfortable. Now it was positively luxurious––a marble reception area, well-furnished courtyard rooms, and a quality restaurant with a fine selection of wines, for which the region is famous. It was designed for the discerning but unadventurous tourist. We didn't need the fancy restaurant; we'd rather experience the town. What we did need were the hot showers and piles of soft towels. We'd done adventurous!

There was nothing like this on Nevado del Acay! Late evening––the ACA overlooked the town–– hundreds of lights sparkled below. Just as people seemed to be retiring and lights went out, fireworks and music began––the start of a local festival. There was a party somewhere in Cachi tonight.

*Cachi*

We were on the last leg. Time now was really short. Plans for Molinos and Cafayate were long gone. What was imperative was to get to Salta and the 2.30 flight to Buenos Aires. Ahead was one of the most spectacular valleys in the Andes, Valle Calchaquí (Enchanted Valley). On desperately poor tyres, we minced our way over another forty miles of broken stone. The valley was breathtaking, but our breath was being held in sympathy with the parlous state of the tyres. The road swooped backwards and forwards down the incredibly steep valley. For miles ahead incredibly tight meanders gradually lost height to the valley floor miles below. The road was narrow. It was early morning. Four-wheel drive vehicles and disturbingly wide luxury coaches brought a fresh crop of tourists for their day in Cachi. We were the only traffic going downhill. Blind corners, precipitous drops of several hundred feet, narrow road, and oncoming coaches were a dangerous combination.

There was little time to watch the scenery, what with the driver concentrating on the road and the passenger concentrating on the driving, but it was spectacular. From the highest point, the road snaked through a dizzy void into the haze of the valley below. Frequent notices reminded us just how 'peligroso' the route was. It was pretty obvious! Still we had to get on, and quickly.

As we descended, the arid grip of the high desert loosened, gradually giving way to luxuriant subtropical vegetation. Grey-blue foliage and pendulous yellow flowers of *Nicotiana glauca* lined the rocky roadside banks. At intervals, intense blue tubular flowers of *Iochroma cyaneum* arched over the road. Finally, approaching the valley floor, trees gave shade, their branches dripping with epiphytic ferns and orchids.

Tarmac at last! Speeding on now, we flew past fertile fields of tobacco and fruit. With less than an hour to check in, we reached the suburbs of Salta. The airport was in sight. Only one last argument with the hire company to slow us down. They seemed unhappy with the Corsa being higher on one corner, tilting drunkenly to one side, and not at all keen to reimburse us for two illegal tyres! We weren't too happy at being marooned and their four failed promises of recovery! We'd no time to prevaricate; agreement was finally reached, to the semi satisfaction of all parties.

Onto the plane. Farewell, Argentina. Europe, here we come!

# The Third Trip
## Salta

After a long week of visiting museums, botanic garden educational projects, attending presentations, advising conservation bodies, and carrying out essential official duties, such as being Honoured by the governing body of Jujuy, we were due some time to explore.

I accepted an invitation to accompany one of the local conservation team the next Saturday morning on a trip, where we would see more of the region. For the plantsman, Argentina is one of the most diverse regions of the world. For the traveller, there are new experiences around almost every corner. I hope this account will give the reader some feeling for this exceptional region.

'Six; Carlos will pick you up at six.' That was six in the morning––not at all my favourite time.

It was six now––pitch-black outside, everyone else snoring, me half asleep (maybe three-quarters)! I made my way to the lobby. No sign of Carlos. Standing by the desk, a tall, dishevelled guy talked to the night porter. He turned towards me. 'John-John, Mr John?'

'Sí,' I said and followed him.

At the kerb, there was a battered pick-up truck. I got in, thinking this wasn't sensible, driving into the night with an unexpected stranger, no idea where we were going, not enough Spanish to communicate effectively, his English almost as limited.

We drove into the dark. 'John-John' seemed to indicate he knew who to pick up, so everything should be OK.

It was a bit disconcerting, but Argentina wasn't a country in which to feel too concerned. If I'd noticed the revolver hanging from his belt, I'd have been more worried.

*Salta at dawn*

Ten minutes later, I'd established his name was Salvador. This wasn't his truck. His car was much more respectable but had broken down. Dawn slowly lightened the sky, and after a while, the surroundings became more familiar. We turned sharply and pulled into a pleasant compound surrounded by traditional timber houses. I'd been here before; dogs surrounded the truck. Carlos emerged in the yellow light of a doorway and welcomed us.

Equipment was thrown into the back of the truck. We sped off. I'd have preferred delay; 6 a.m. was far too early for breakfast. It would have been very welcome now. So *sin* breakfast, we were off fishing, fly fishing for trout in a desert to be precise.

As barking dogs faded, three of us tried, without much success, to settle comfortably into two seats in a space inconveniently interrupted by a gear stick. For a while, we drove alongside the wide dry riverbed of the Rio Grande. A feeble stream of permanent water gave no indication of the occasional power of a raging river that drained the Yungas. The width of the valley provided ample evidence, as did bleached tumbled stones, worn smooth by millennia of flash floods. Below the road, a bridge spanned the wide valley. We took a right turn and sped over the bridge leading into a side valley.

Smooth black road was gone. This happens in South America. As we bounced through ruts, stones rattled around the wheel arches. A switchback of a road took us high above the river. I ignored the vertical drop to the left and the immediacy of the nearside wheels to the precipice.

It was an oddly luxuriant place; incredibly rich vegetation hid steep slopes rising 1,000 metres above us. The hills wrung rain from the rising clouds. Rainfall tightly confined to a narrow strip of winding valleys gave the Yungas a unique ecosystem. Beyond the valleys, sometimes as close as the opposite slope, sensitive forest exposed to the drying sun was sparse and dry, rapidly giving way to the ubiquitous arid desert conditions of the north-west. But here bromeliads abounded, orchids clothed the trees, strange (*Rhipsalis*) cacti snaked down their trunks, and birds and insects filled the air.

*Contrasting slopes in the Yungas*

It soon became clear that this was not to be a short trip into the foothills. On and on we went, further and further from paved roads and civilisation. The truck was elderly and unsuited for this type of travel. But that wasn't unusual here. It wouldn't normally have bothered me, but it brought back memories of a similar Argentinian journey just a year earlier involving a distressed vehicle, two flat tyres, and a 6,000-metre mountain pass!

Passing several likely fishing spots, after nearly twenty kilometres, we pulled onto a grassy clearing closely grazed by sheep and goats. A crude timber and cable suspension footbridge confirmed that people were around. A few small farms were tucked out of sight into the wooded fringes above the river.

It was around this time that Carlos told me that cannibals had lived here. Uniquely for Argentina, apparently only in this valley, an aboriginal tribe led a cannibal lifestyle. Fortunately for us, the past tense applied. The Conquistadores had wiped them out four hundred years earlier, but for a while, Spanish evangelists were a sought-after delicacy.

Carlos grabbed a bundle of rods from the back of the truck and handed me one. It was a light river rod that had seen far better days, in its prime for the job. But now the first joint was insecurely taped up with Sellotape.

Reels were located and a floating line selected. Armed with a modest selection of flies we set off. Where was the river? To reach it there was a chasm to negotiate. It wasn't a mighty chasm by Andes standards, just a five-foot gap, where the bank had been eroded. It wasn't that wide, but there was a drop just inconvenient enough to guarantee at least one broken leg. No problem––jump.

Safely negotiated, I cast across a pool. Half a dozen casts later, crack! Sellotape has no place in the rod repair trade.

I called Carlos. No problem; he'd use this rod. I'd use his. A telescopic bait rod fitted with a fly line wouldn't satisfy traditionalists, but it was possible to cast a short line with reasonable accuracy.

Carlos moved upstream, gesturing for me to follow. Stumbling over the tumbled stones that made up the dry riverbed was tricky and slow. Every few hundred metres we waded across shallow, very cold water. There was no point trying to keep dry. It was unpleasant at first but became welcome as we walked into the increasingly intense sun. I kept walking. Carlos walked much more quickly. No matter. To fish you have to pause, frequently. I'd soon catch up.

But Carlos didn't pause. He strode ahead, gradually gaining ground, in no time just a tiny figure in the distance. He was half a kilometre ahead, fast disappearing around a bend in the river. It was a scene like a filmmaker's fantasy of Neanderthal hunters strung out across an ancient landscape. But this wasn't the Stone Age. This was now.

Suddenly, a surprisingly powerful wind sprung up. Dense dry dust swirled down the valley, confined by the cliffs on either side. Walking backwards kept dust from the eyes but did nothing for speed. Carlos was gone. Salvador had also disappeared. I was uneasy again. OK. I could walk back to the truck. It was only three kilometres downstream. I was keen to go on but very thirsty. Skipping breakfast hadn't helped my energy levels. If my guides sidestepped into a tributary, it wouldn't be easy to find them. I fished as I walk, a few casts here and there. No takes, not a sign of fish except a few small fry in the shallows.

With Carlos striding out towards Chile, I shouted for him to stop. Stop he did, eventually, a tiny figure in the distance. I caught up. Whilst I drew breath, Carlos took a dried leaf from a pouch and chewed it. Coca! Was this his secret? No need for breakfast if you have traditional Andean stimulants!

*Five kilometres upriver*

Drinks?

'Drink the river. The mountain water's clean,' he said.

Unsure if I had the gut flora to cope with South American rivers, I sipped a little. We walked on. A conical hill rose ahead.

'Beyond the hill, there's a pool. We'll fish there.'

Another kilometre, no sign of the pool. It was hot. It was dry. That was enough!

Four hours walking, five kilometres upriver, no fish. Forget fish. They weren't nearly as interesting as the fantastic surroundings. Clasped within the grasp of 200-foot-high cliffs we looked up into a perfect blue sky. Turkey vultures wheeled above. In the riverine scrub, a tree was loaded with spherical black fruits. Sweet and aromatic, they had a distinct taste of strawberries. Myrtaceae. Closer identification would have to wait. They turned out to be *Myrtus communis*, a plant once well known in Victorian wedding bouquets! Sudden high thin whistles and whirring wings announced the arrival of three hummingbirds engaged in a territorial dispute.

Just above head height, just beyond the reach of grazing animals, huge apple green bromeliad rosettes, fully a metre high, clung precariously to the vertical cliffs. From their centres, candy-pink flower spikes arched out, doubling their size. Protruding from the spikes, contrasting indigo-blue flowers dispensed nectar to the patrolling hummingbirds. Dense clumps of spiky *Abromeitiella* hugged the loose cliff face. Something caught my eye; there was something red at the centre of a clump.

At last! The glistening scarlet flowers of *Rebutia* sp., a finely spined, globular cactus that had evaded us for the last week. Once the target had been detected, they erupted everywhere, all in flower.

It's funny how this happens. It must be a primitive hunting skill. It's difficult to find the first individual, but once it's been located, our eyes become 'laser guided.' We focus only on our current obsession.

My fellow traveller would be furious. As a non-fisherman and world cactus expert, he'd had the pleasure of a 'lie-in' and a late departure to an educational workshop. But I'd found the *Rebutia*. He'd really missed out!

*(Rebutia)*

We retraced our steps. A group of cormorants moved politely out of the way as we passed. We'd had trouble finding fish, but they didn't. It was hard to see how they hunted in the shallow water; they must outmaneuver fish in the deeper sections and pools. We were no competition; they barely acknowledged our presence. Settling on a nearby sandbar, they hung their wings out to dry like five miniature scarecrows.

Maybe we couldn't find fish, but we did find tadpoles. As our shadows fell over the warm edges of pools, thousands of glistening black shapes wriggled into the silt and completely disappeared.

There was another bird––one of the great birds of the Andes. It wasn't a condor or an eagle. It didn't have a nine-foot wingspan. It was a duck! Not the one you throw bread at in your local park.

This is the Peruvian torrent duck. For a duck, it's pretty striking. Females are blue grey above, chestnut beneath. The males sport a trendy black-and-white-striped head. Several times as we walked, a single drake would fly off, fast and low, over the water, to quieter surroundings.

Its fancy plumage isn't its claim to fame; its name tells all. This odd bird is found the length of the Andes, from Venezuela to Terra del Fuego. Find fast flowing rivers, and you'll find torrent ducks. Nothing matches the torrent ducks' ability to conquer the strongest currents. Their secret––a rudder-like tail equipped with a bunch of stiff quills that help them steer through the fastest mountain torrents. Newborn ducklings follow their parents upstream against the rushing water, seeming almost to run across the surface.

## Asado

At last we regained our starting point. We stopped on a sunny gravel spit against the far bank. Flat river-polished stones were great makeshift seating––'great' until I lifted one and a spider the size of my hand glared up at me. It seemed to my nonexpert eye to look worryingly like the Brazilian wandering spider, one of the most venomous spiders in the world.

*Unwelcome surprise*

Composed again, we relaxed in the welcome shade of the overhanging bank. Salvador had assembled a fire of driftwood, and Carlos had begun butchering a sack full of beef and lamb. Smoke from the asado announced lunch was on the way. In this land of beef, it was even possible to tire of steak. But when it was straight from the fire, flavoured by the aromatic smoke of *Prosopis* wood, there'd be no leftovers.

Back in the car, we retraced our route, long and incredibly bumpy on the unmade road. As we bounced along, Salvador had trouble keeping the car in gear. It seemed to have ambitions of becoming an automatic but had only reached the stage of slipping into neutral. Salvador seemed to be more perturbed than this minor mechanical indiscipline should cause and conferred mysteriously with Carlos.

Ten miles, further over arid ruts, we stopped unexpectedly. Carlos and Salvador lifted the hood, and steam billowed out. Mystery no more! A search among the pile of fishing gear, and a makeshift container was located. The radiator was swiftly refilled with water from a swampy ditch.

This did the trick. In no time we were back at the hotel, now bathed in the warm light of late afternoon. No gun discharged, no fish caught. Cold beers could not have been more welcome. Fish suppers would wait!

Printed in the United States
By Bookmasters